GROVE PRESS

New York

TULSA

CLARK

Published simultaneously in Canada
Printed in the United States of America

Library of Congress Cataloging-in-Publication Data
Clark, Larry, 1943–
     Tulsa / Clark.
        p.   cm.
     Originally published: New York : Lustrum Press, c1971.
     ISBN 978-0-8021-1677-2 (hardcover)
     ISBN 978-0-8021-1678-9 (limited edition)
     ISBN 978-0-8021-3748-7 (paperback)
     1. Narcotic addicts—Oklahoma—Tulsa—Pictorial works. I. Title.

   HV5833.T8 C56 2000
   779'.93061—dc21
                                              00-030881

Typography by Dean Bornstein

Grove Press
An Imprint of Grove Atlantic
154 West 14th Street,
New York, NY 10011.
17 18 10 9 8 7

Thanks to my friends Ralph Gibson and Danny Seymour for their help with
this book.

i was born in tulsa oklahoma in 1943. when i was
sixteen i started shooting amphetamine. i shot
with my friends everyday for three years and then
left town but i've gone back through the years.
once the needle goes in it never comes out.

L.C.

1963

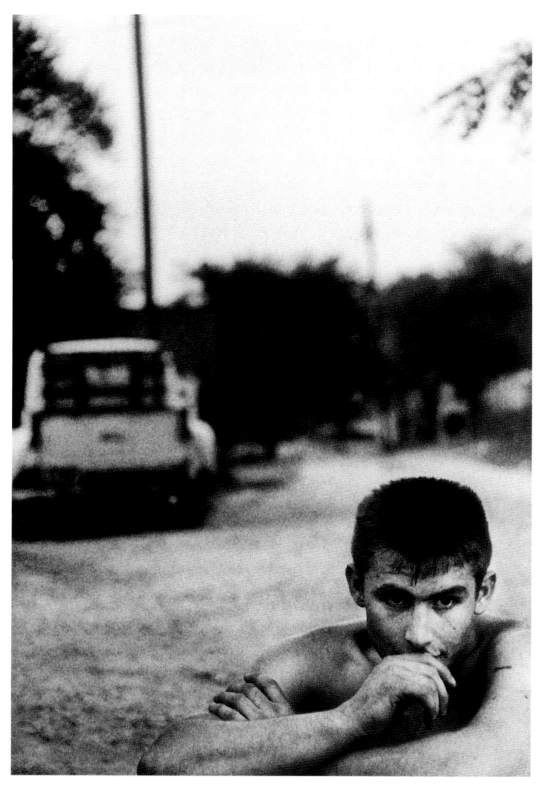

david roper

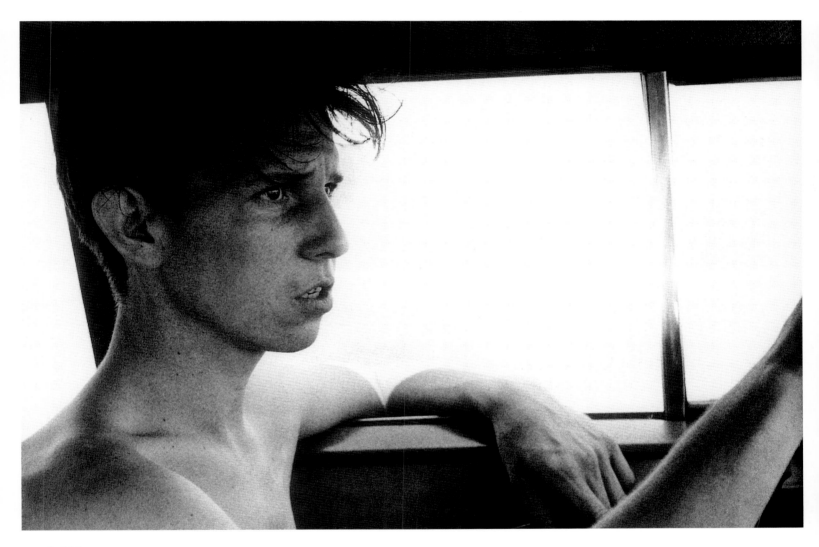

billy mann

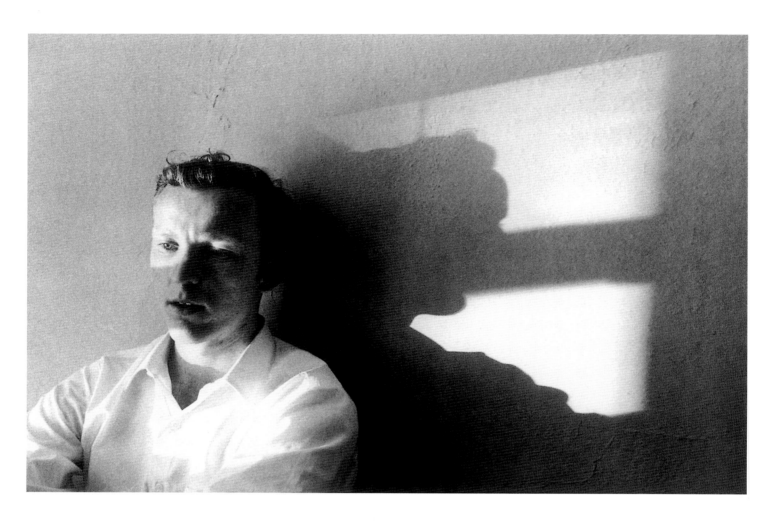

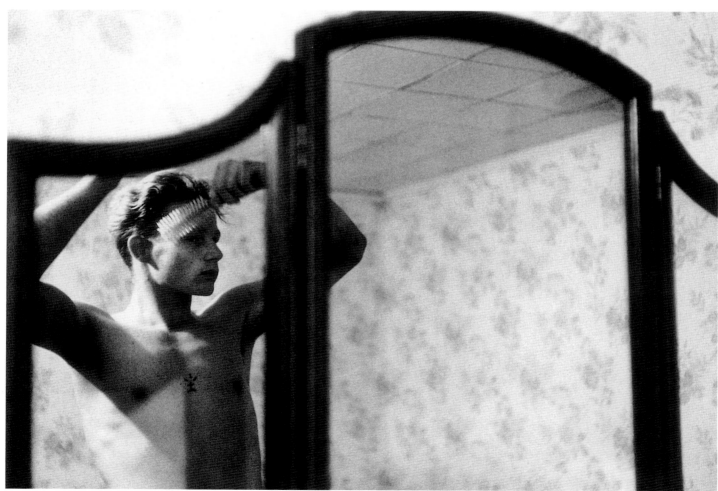

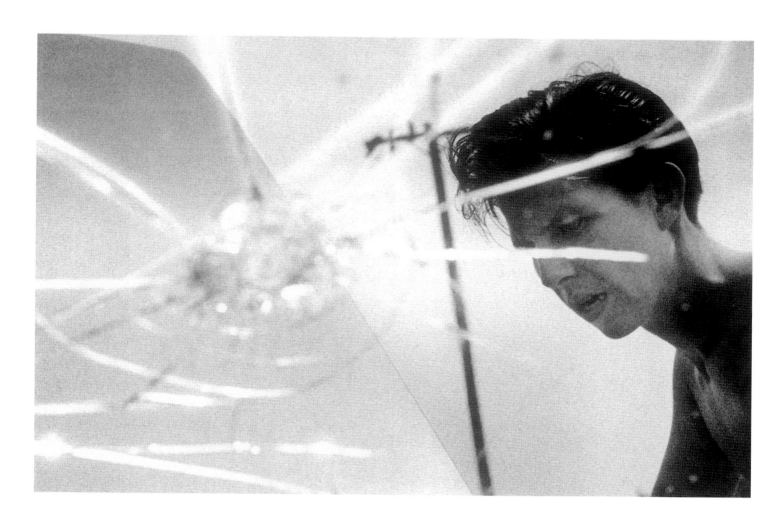

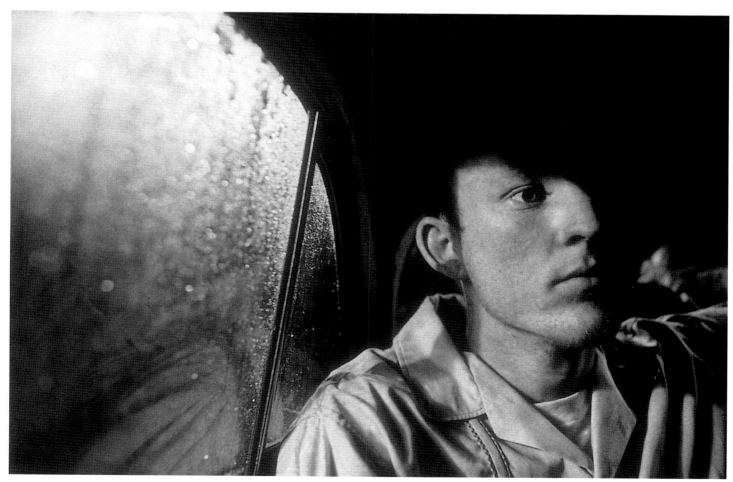

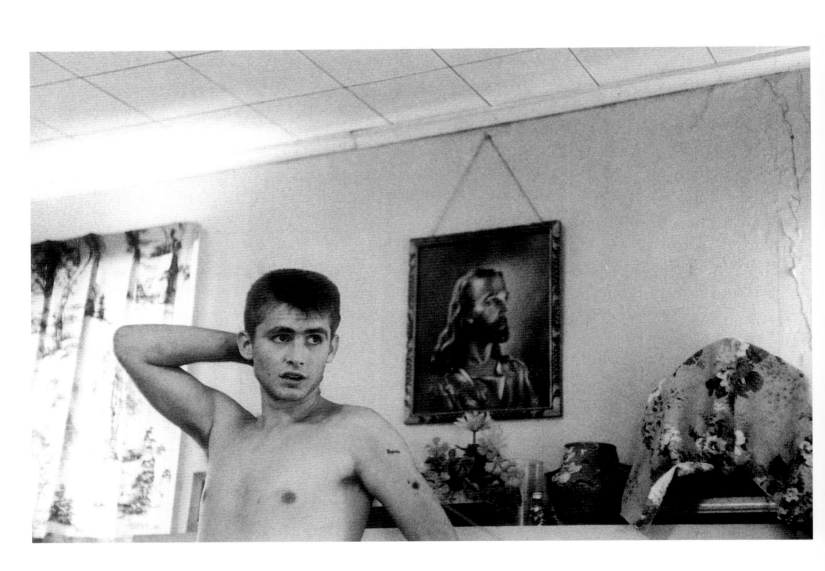

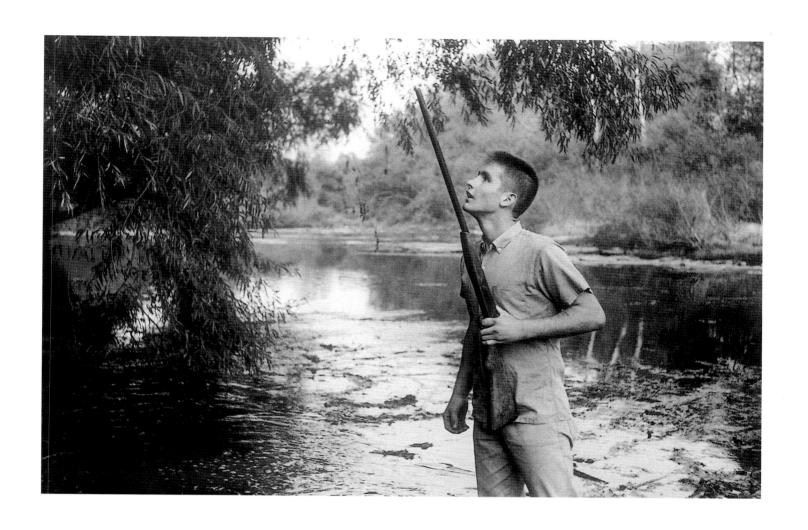

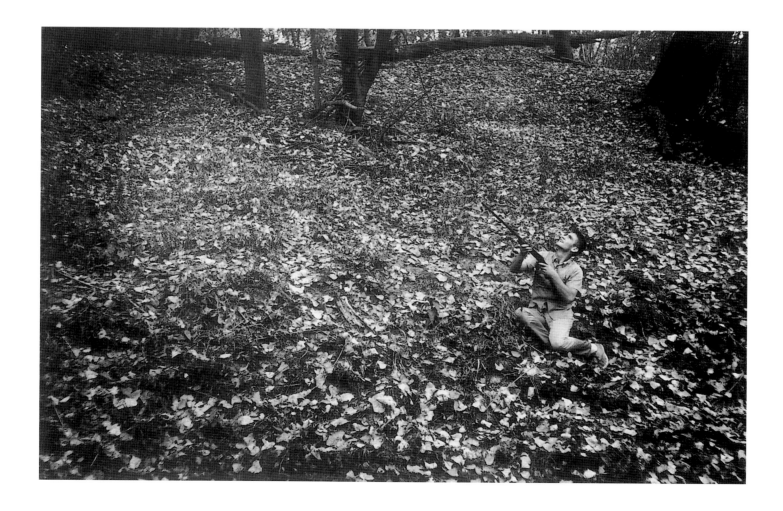

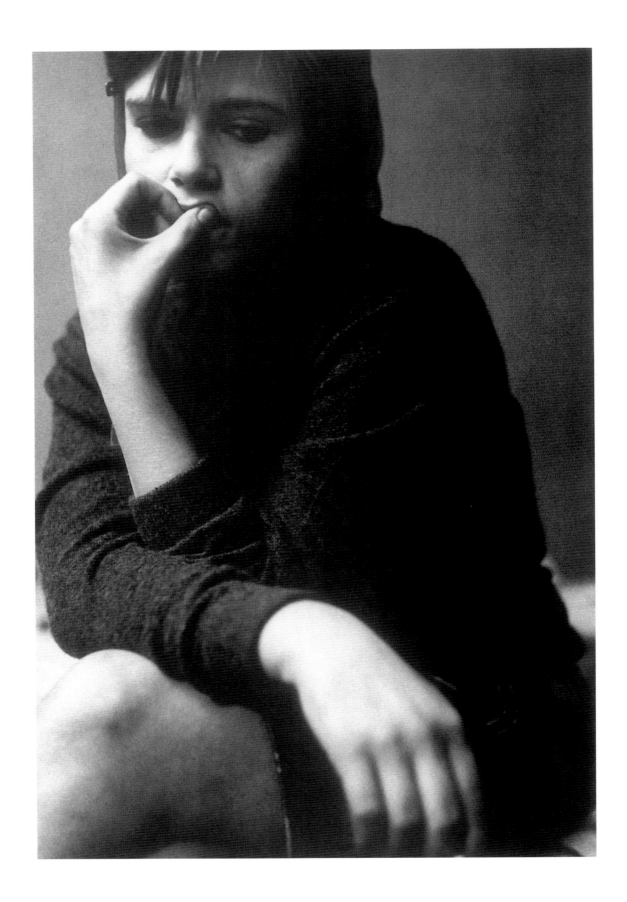

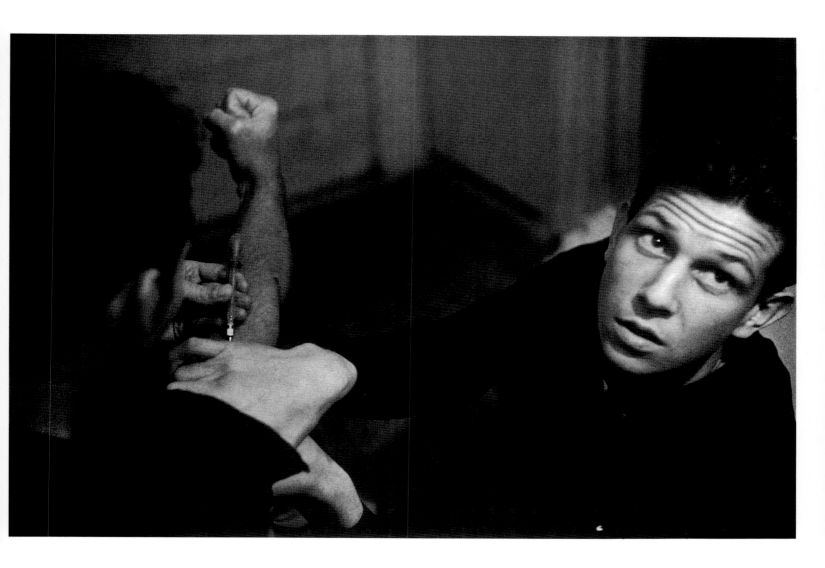

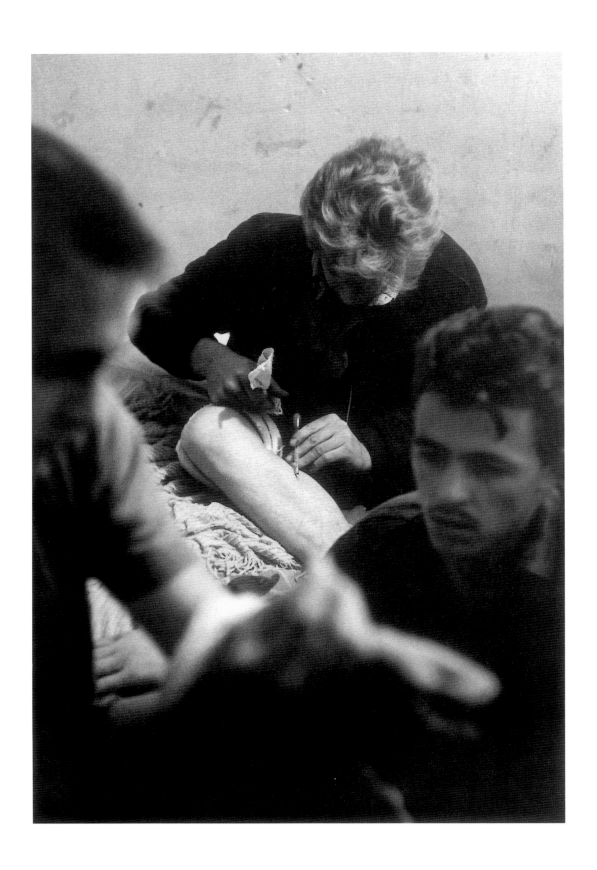

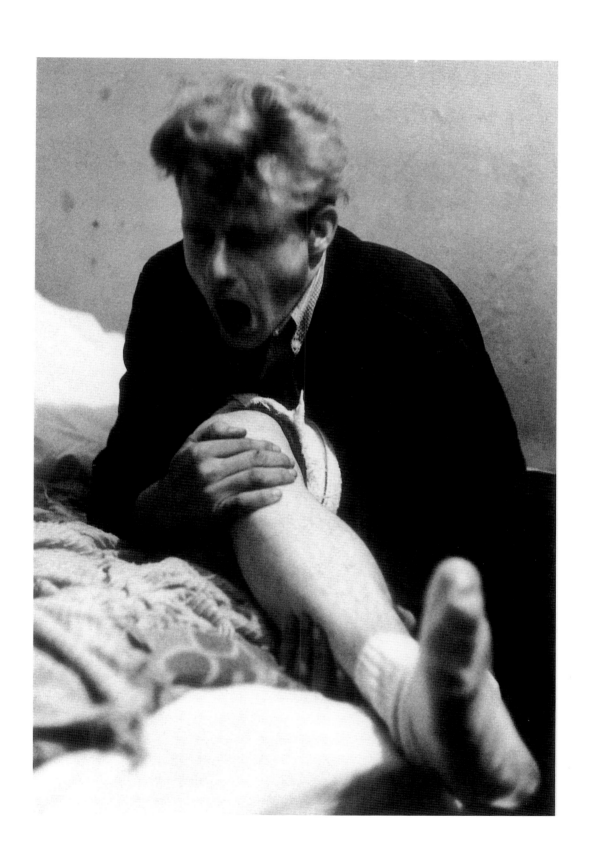

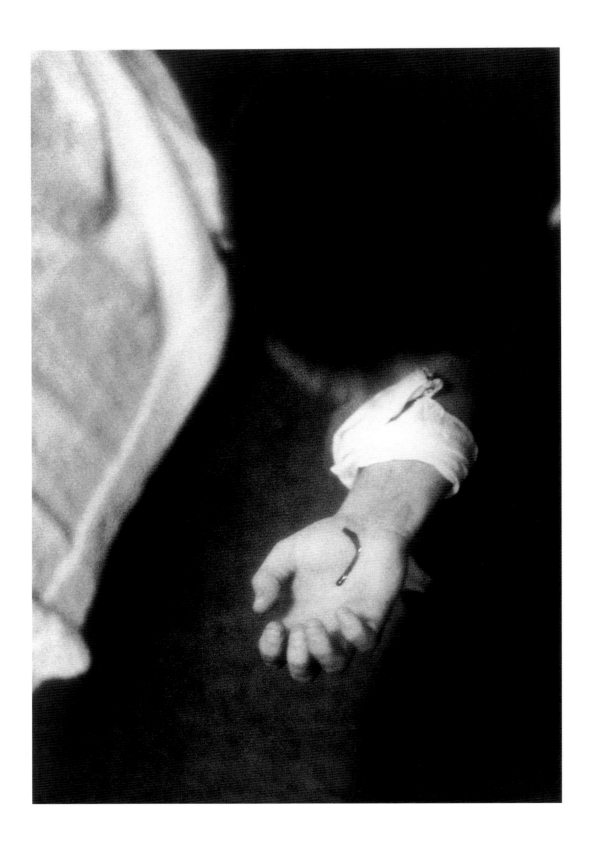

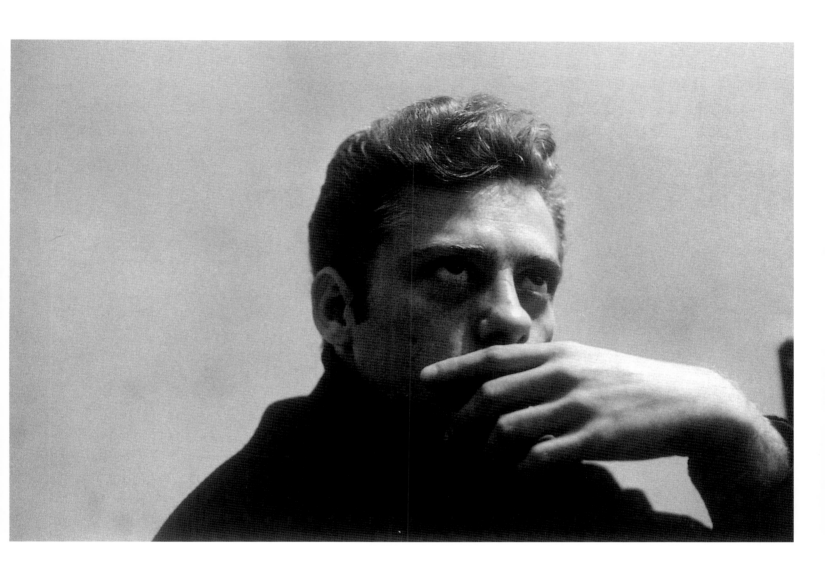

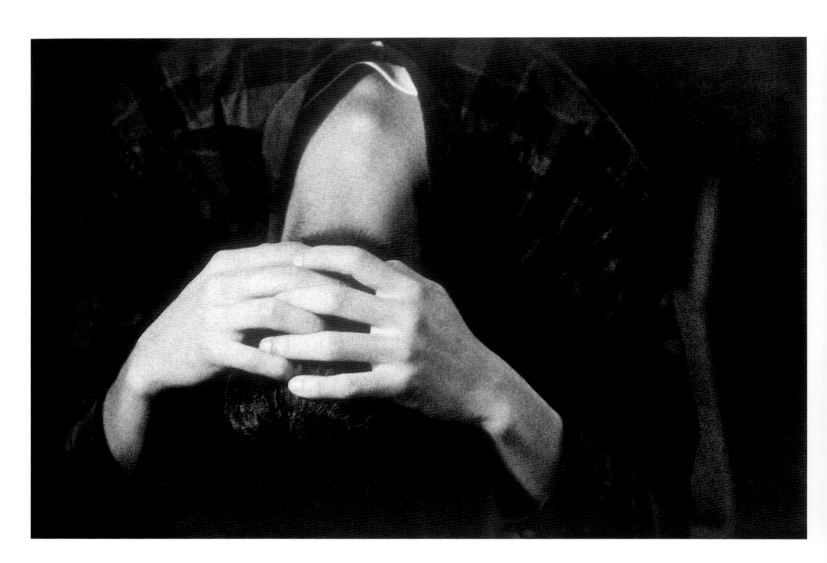

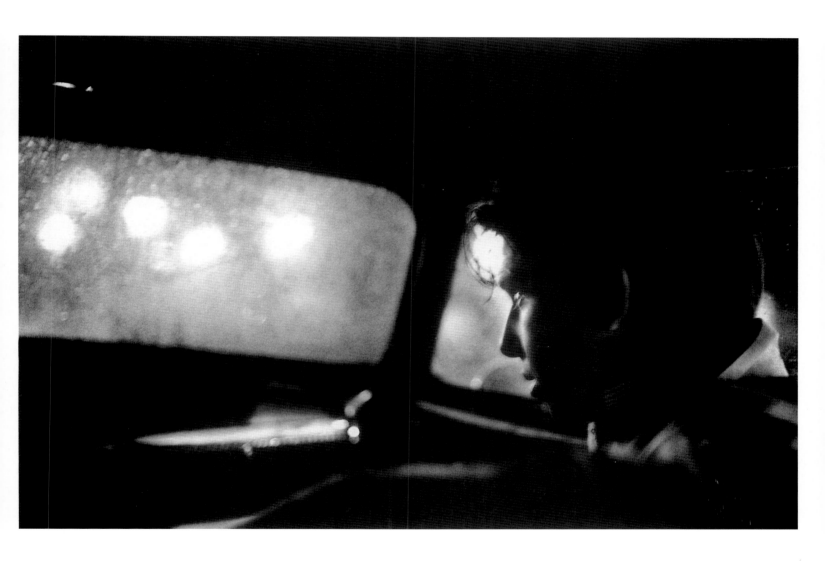

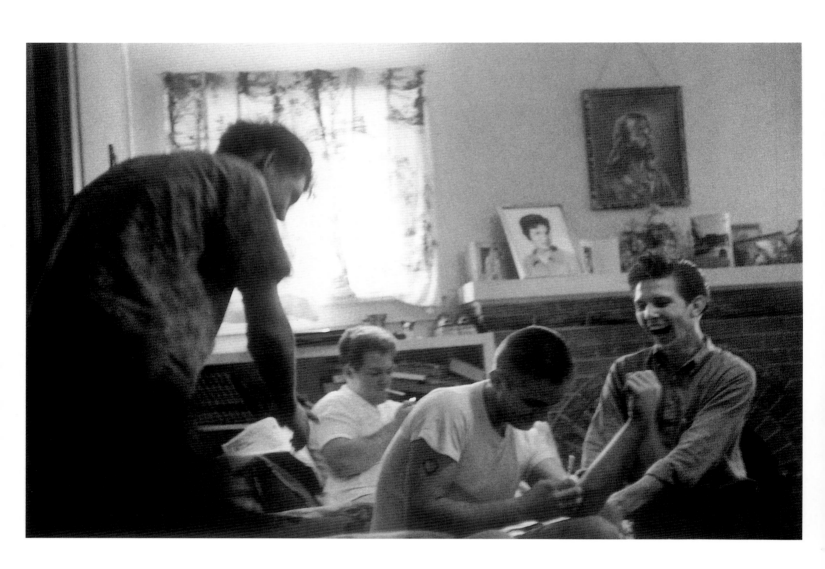

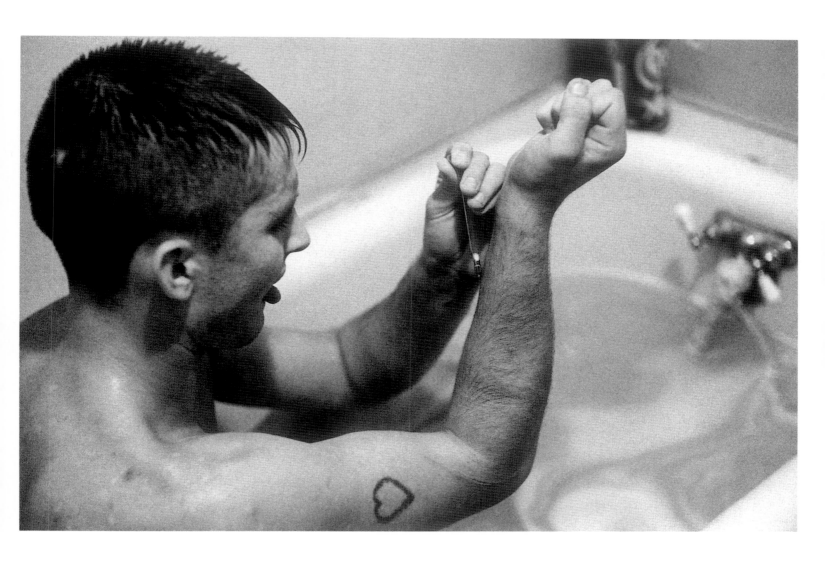

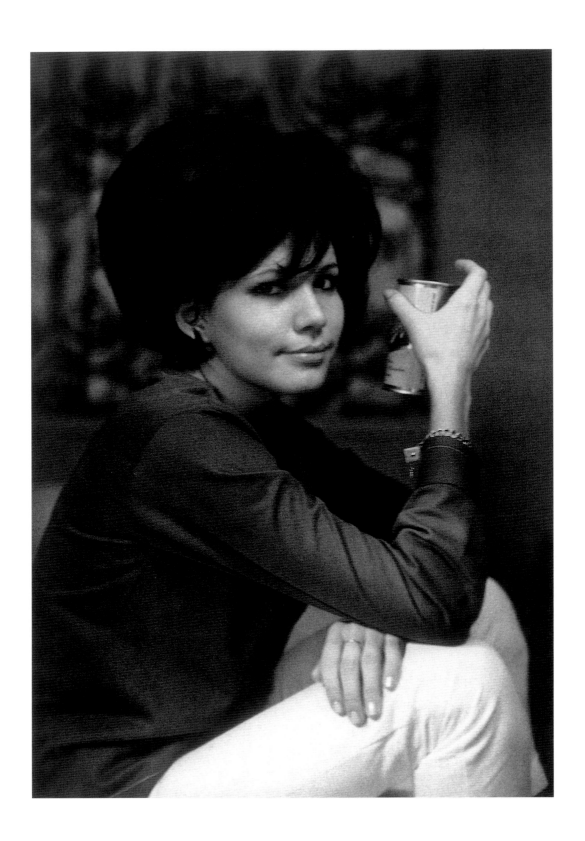

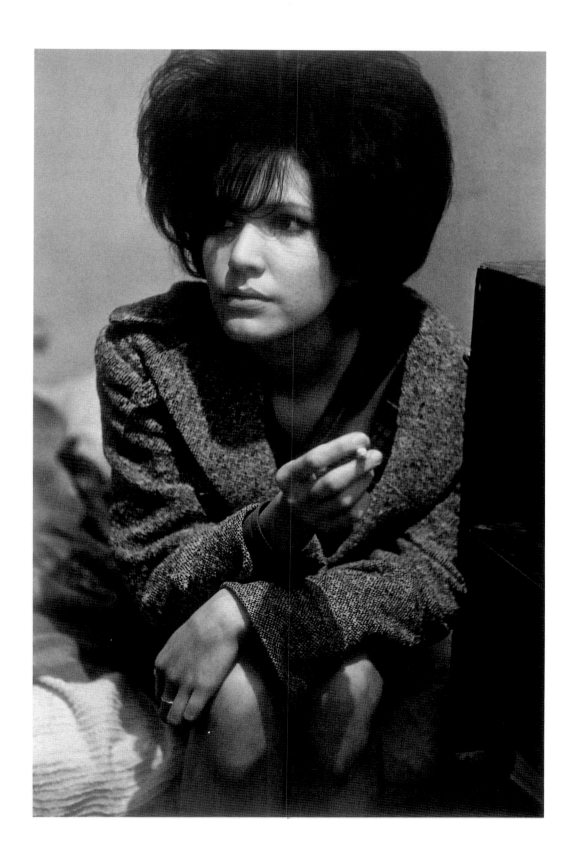

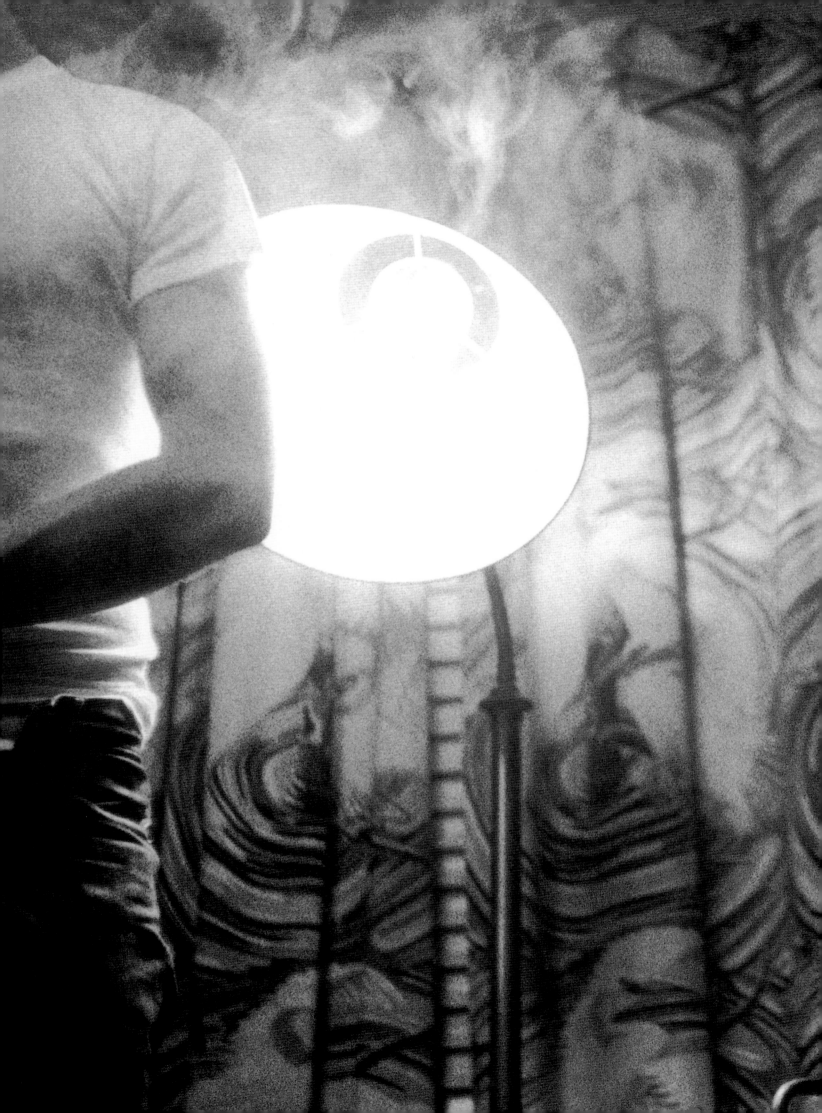

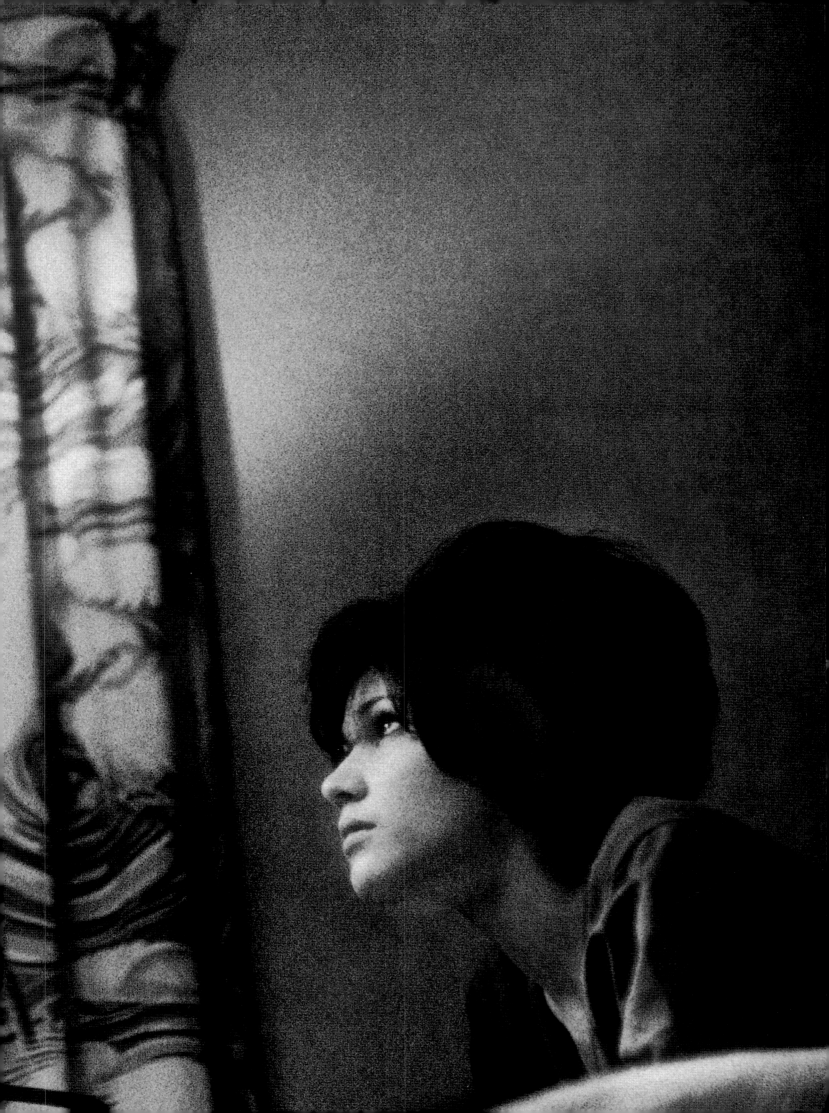

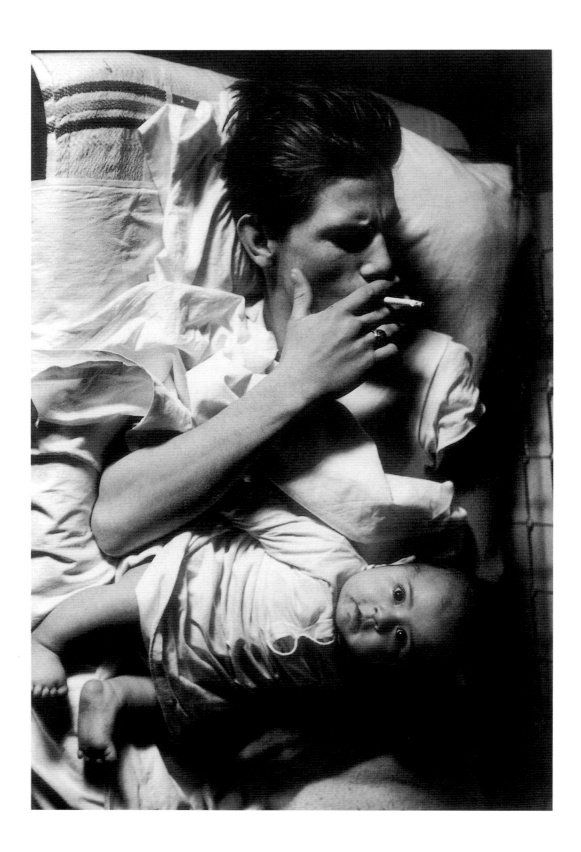

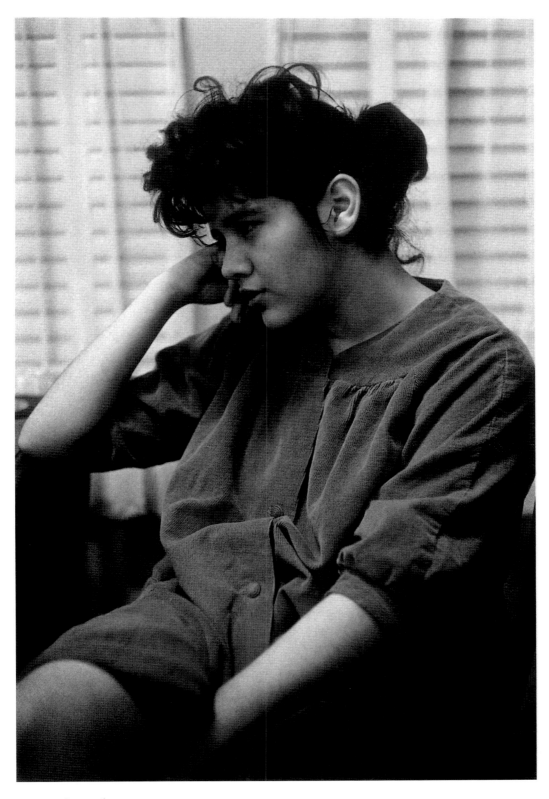

dead

1968

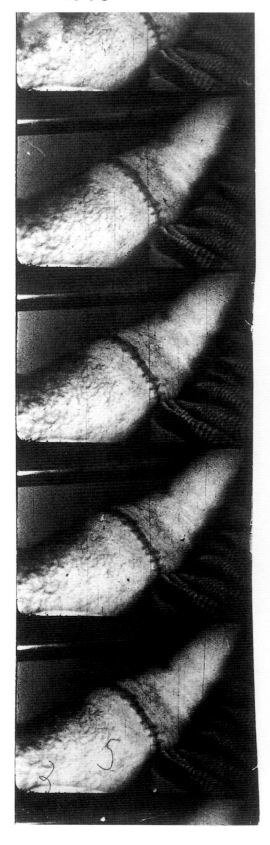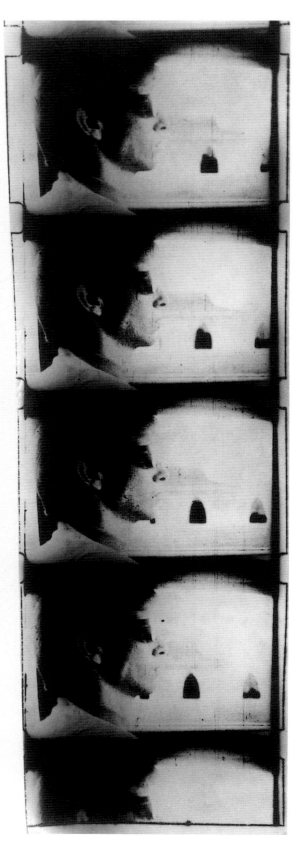

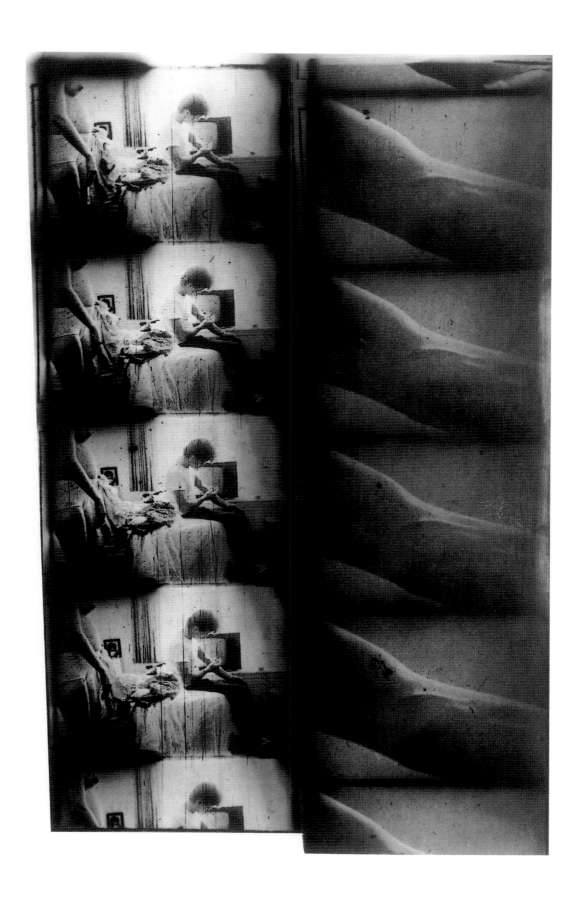

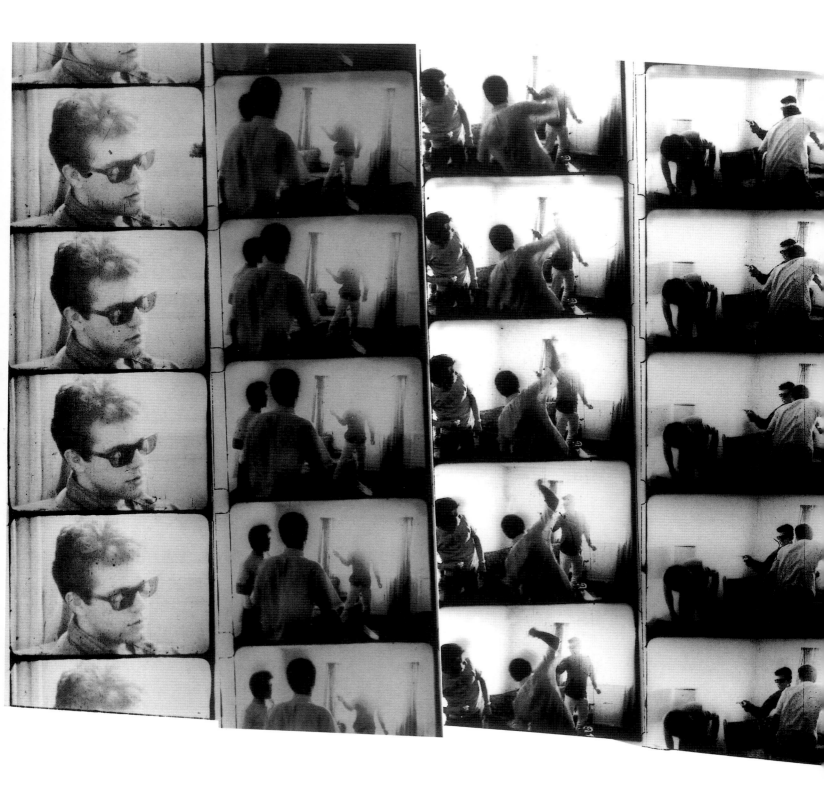

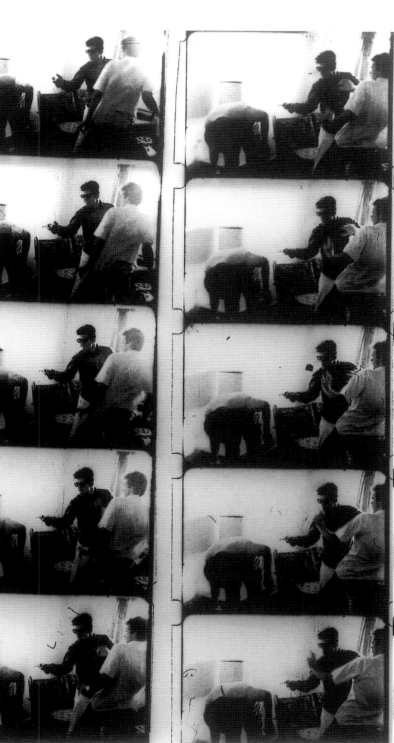
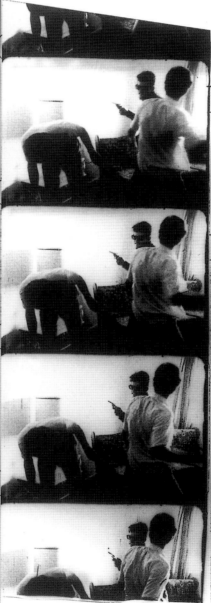
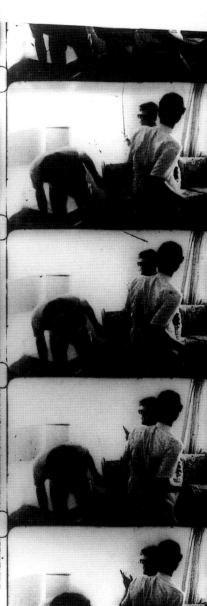

death is more perfect than life

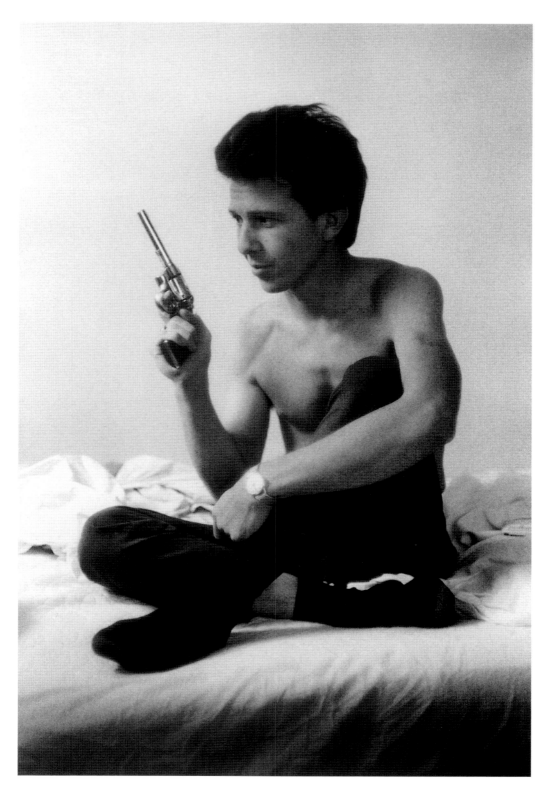

dead 1970

1971

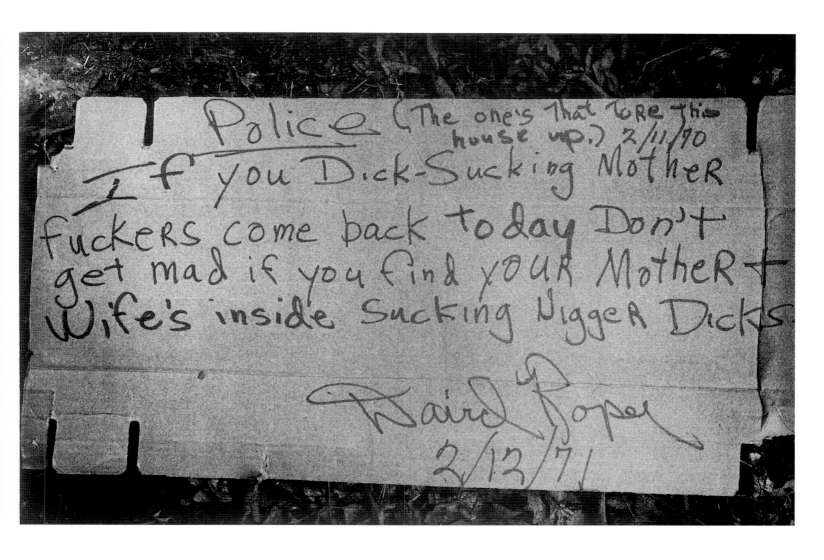

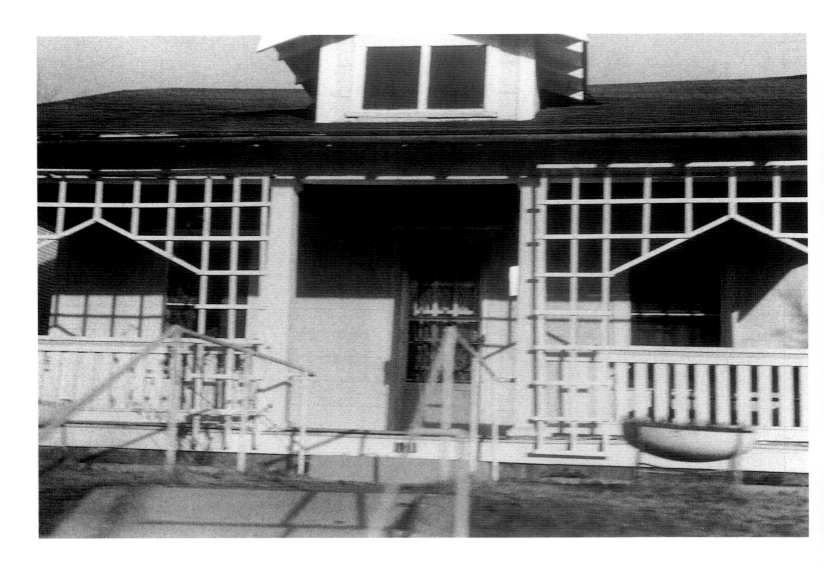

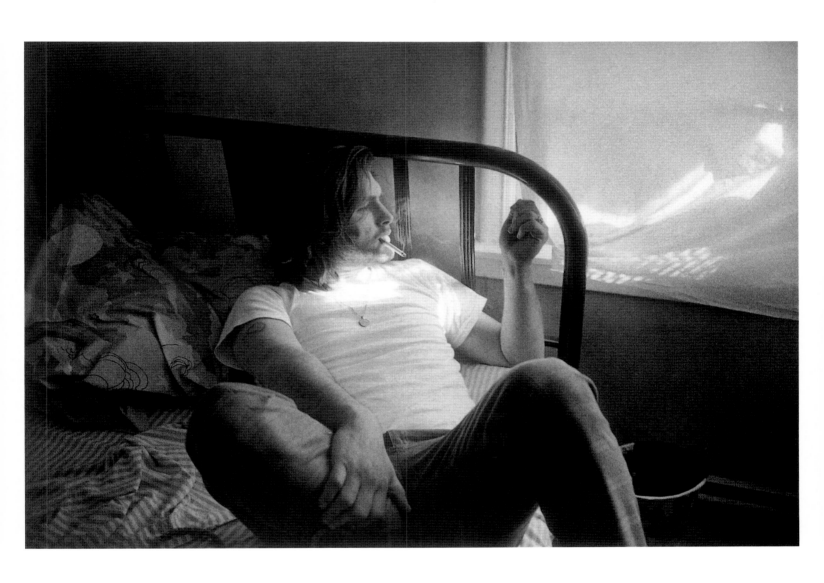

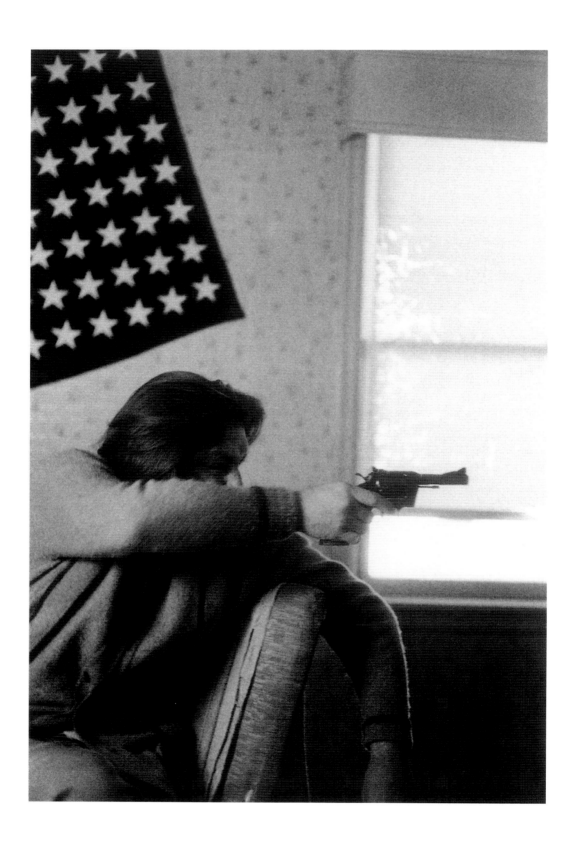

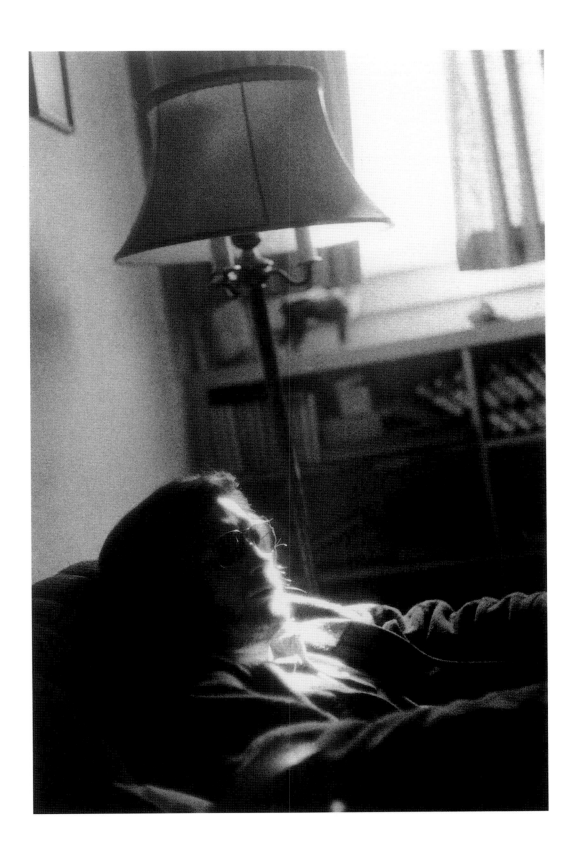

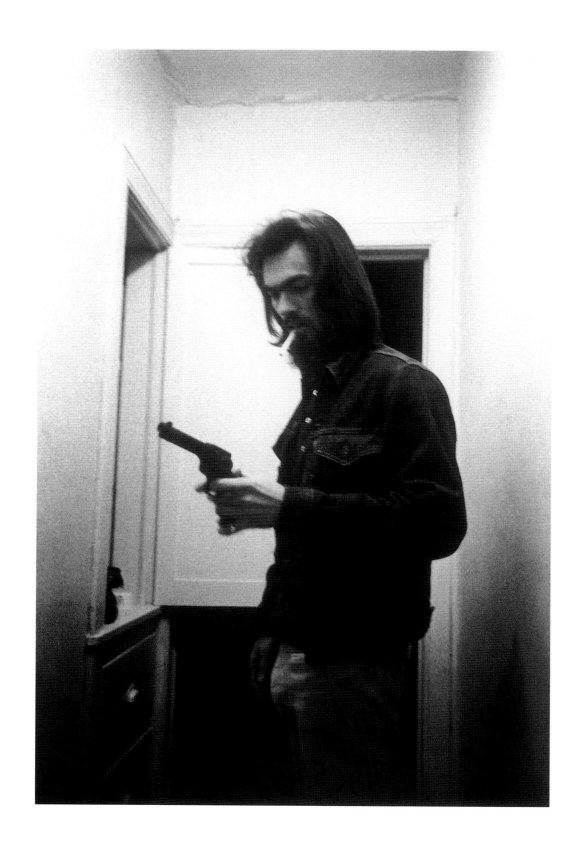

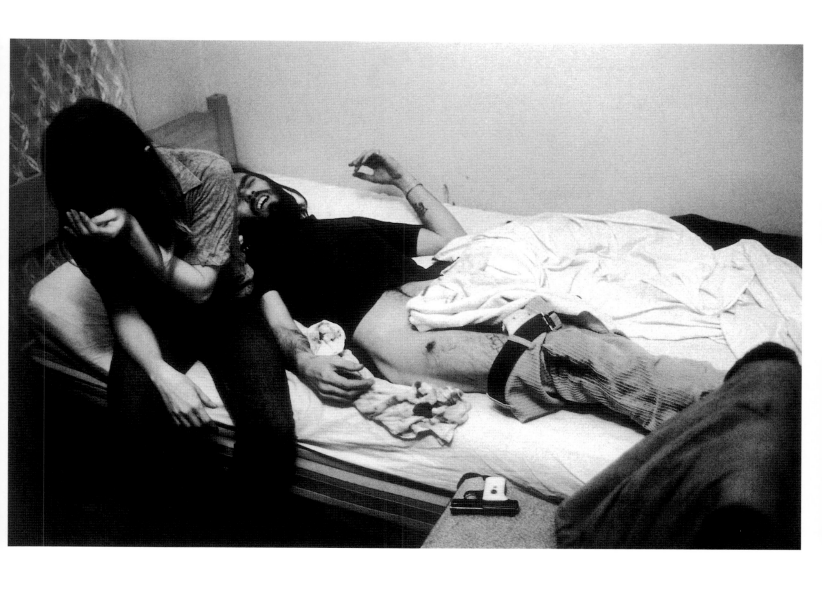

accidental gunshot wound

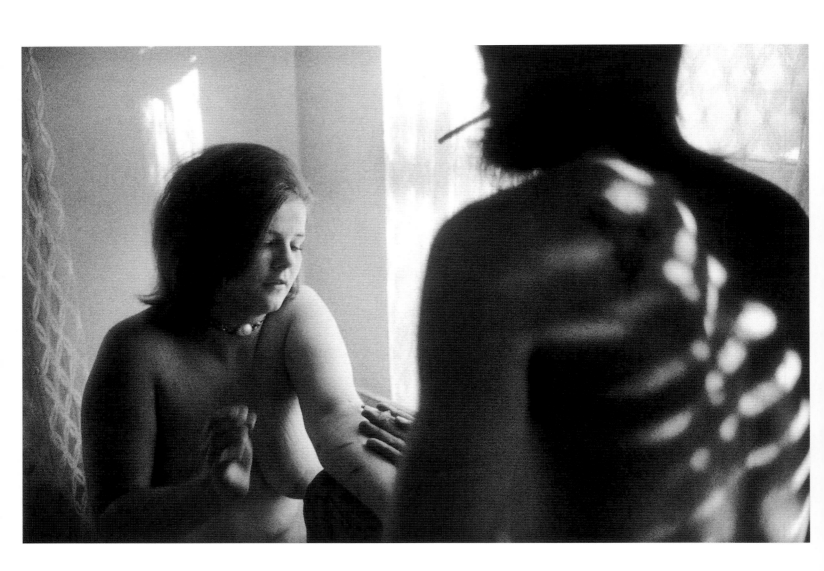

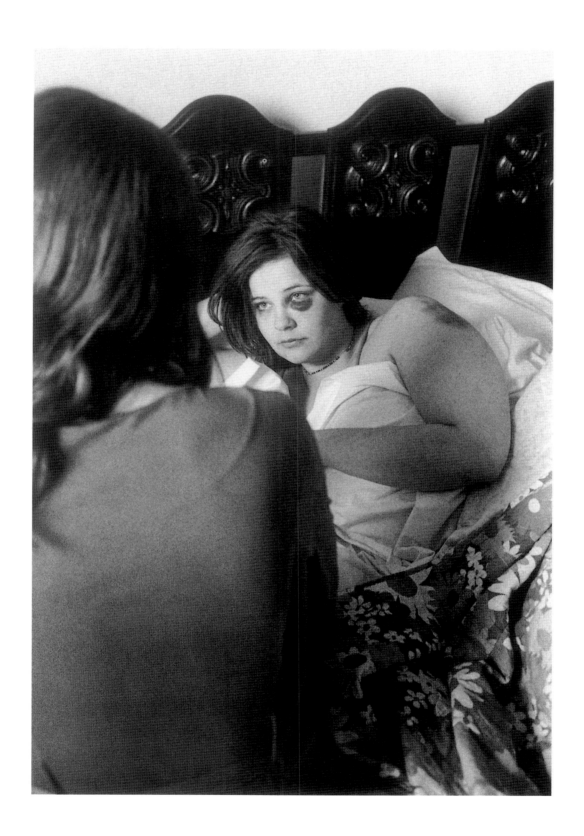

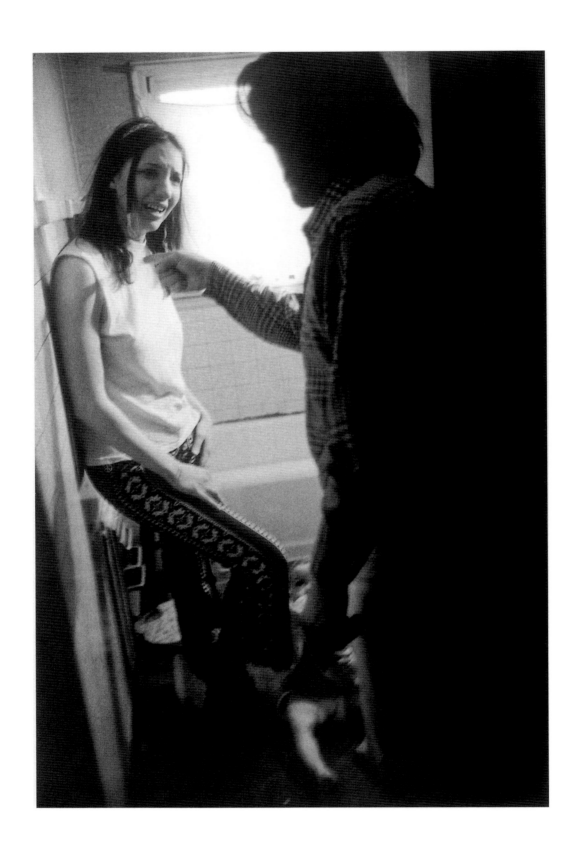

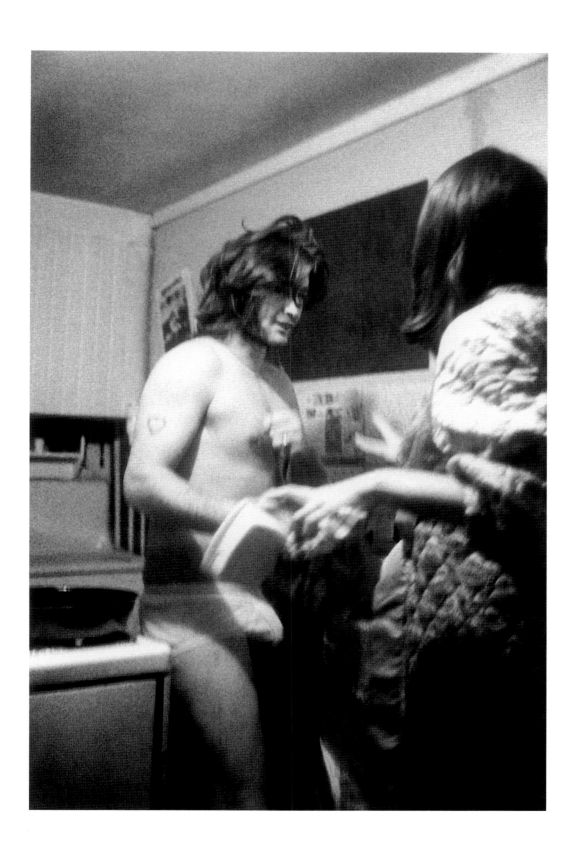

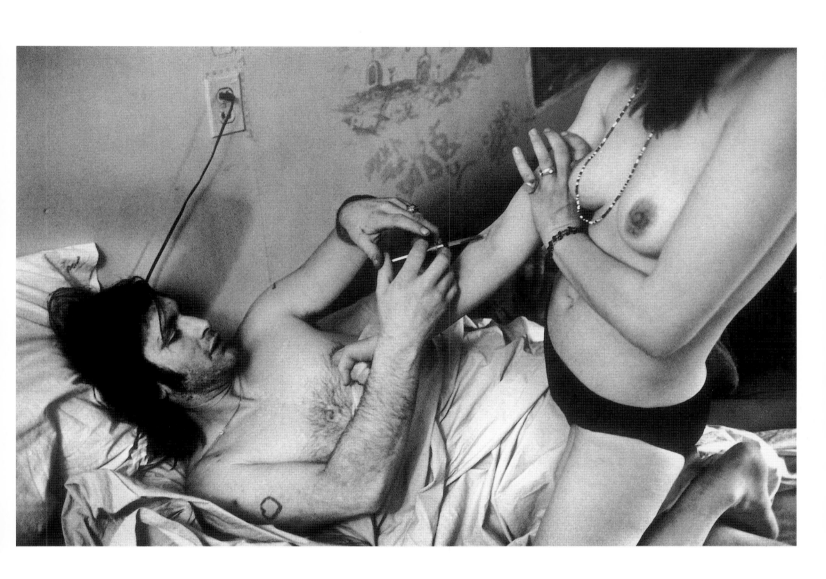

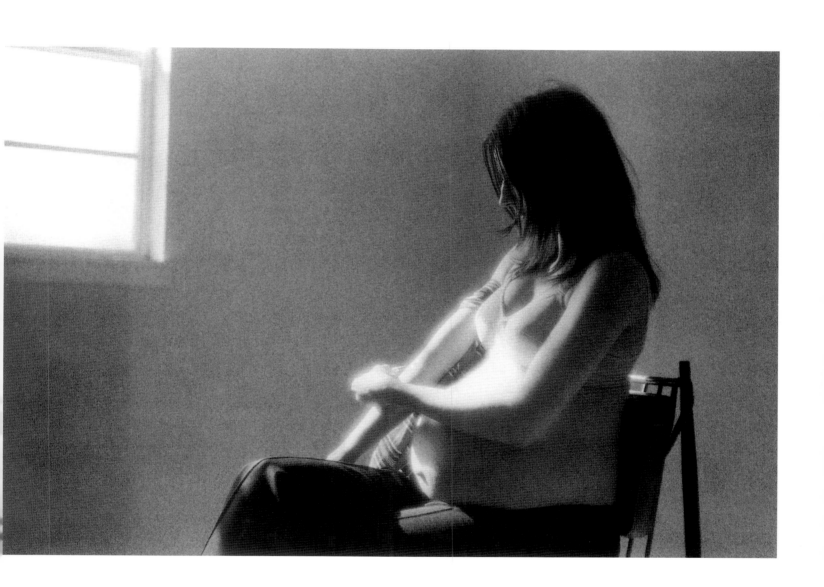

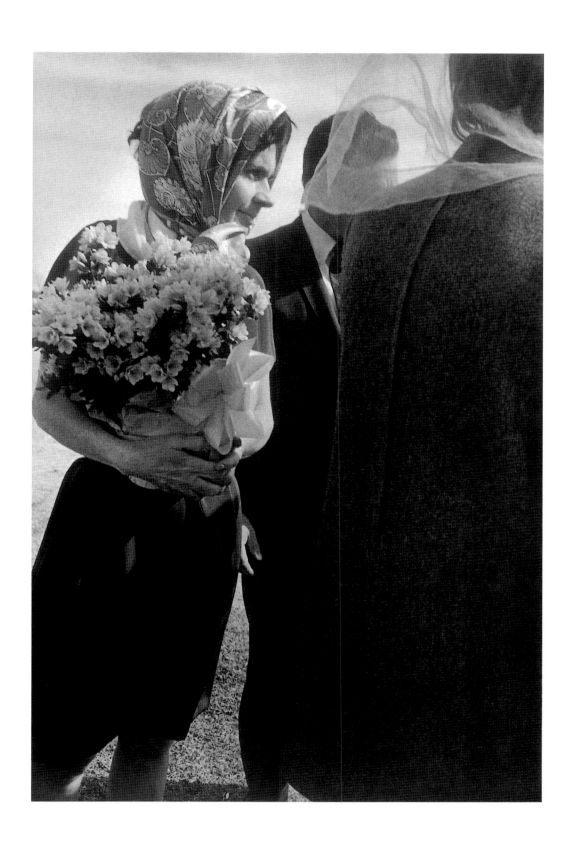

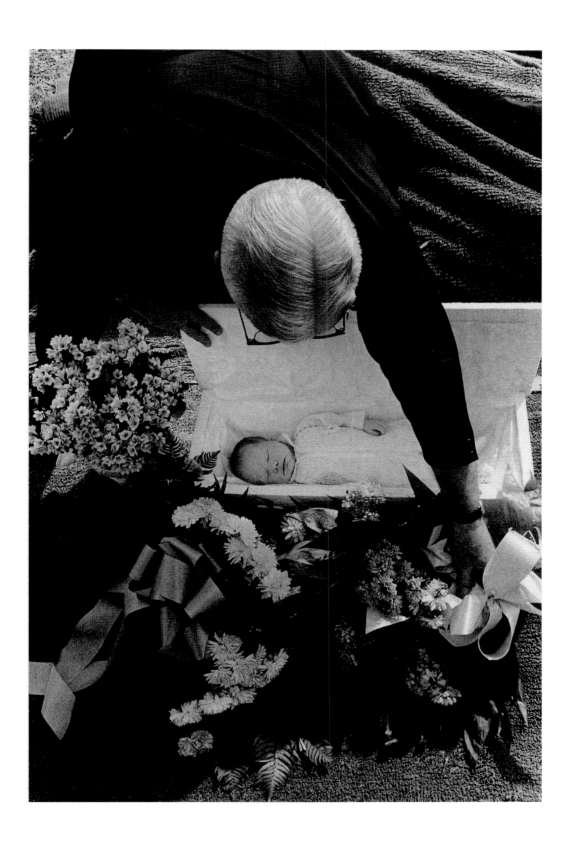

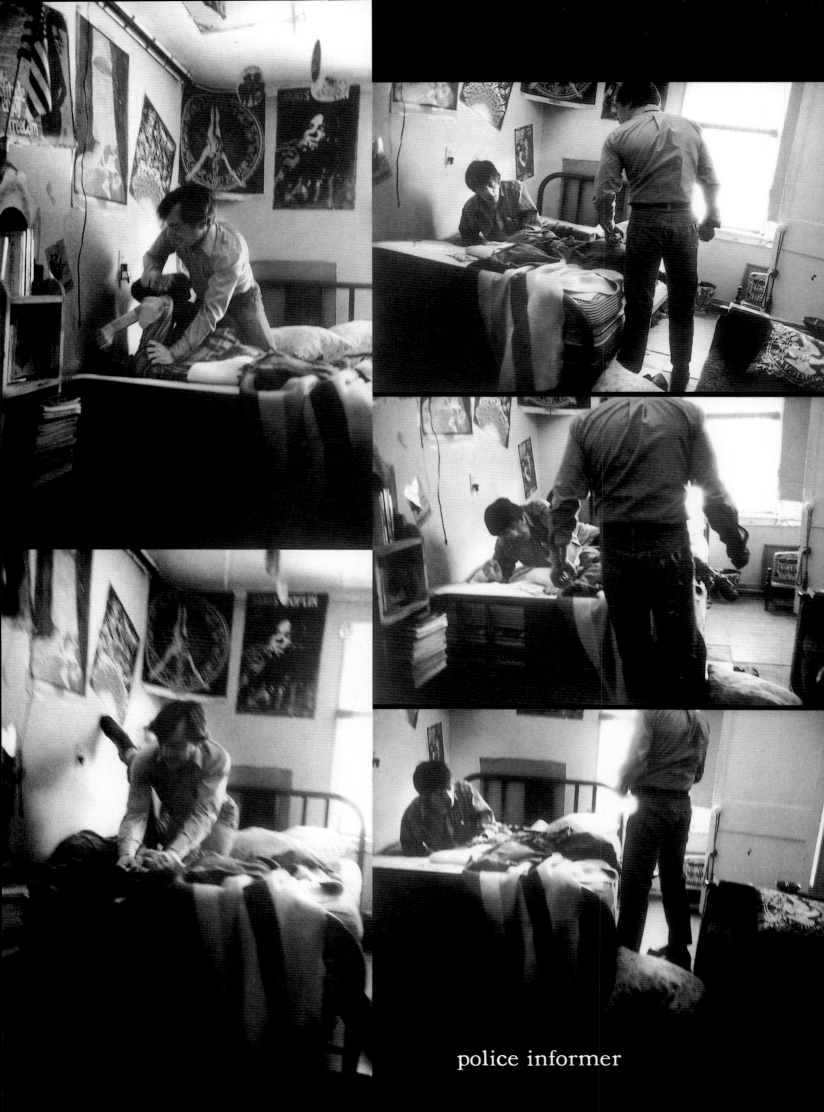

police informer

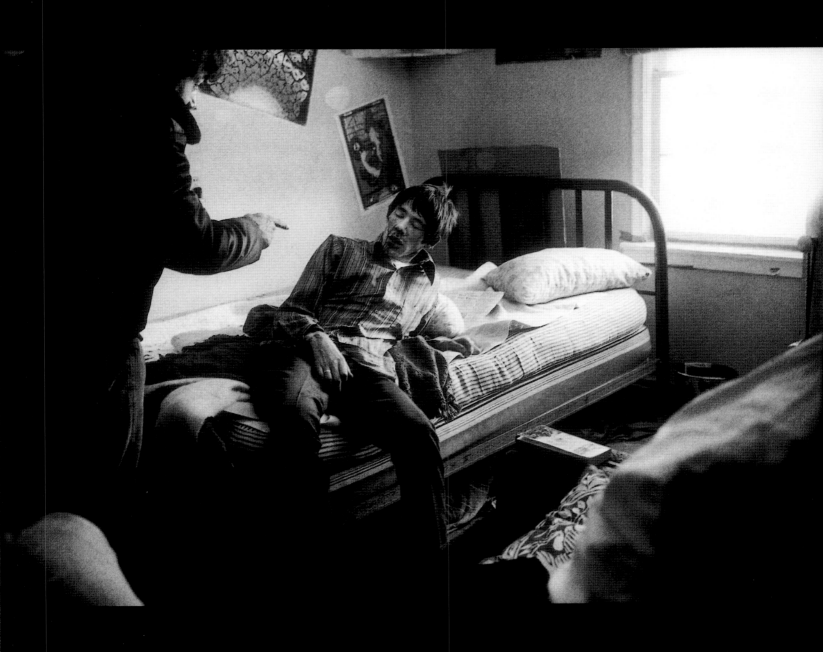

everytime i see you punk you're gonna get the same

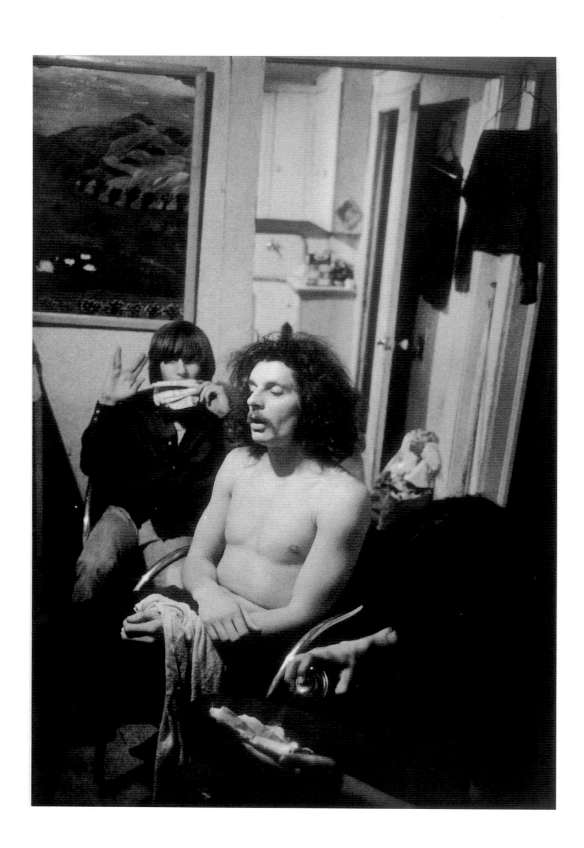

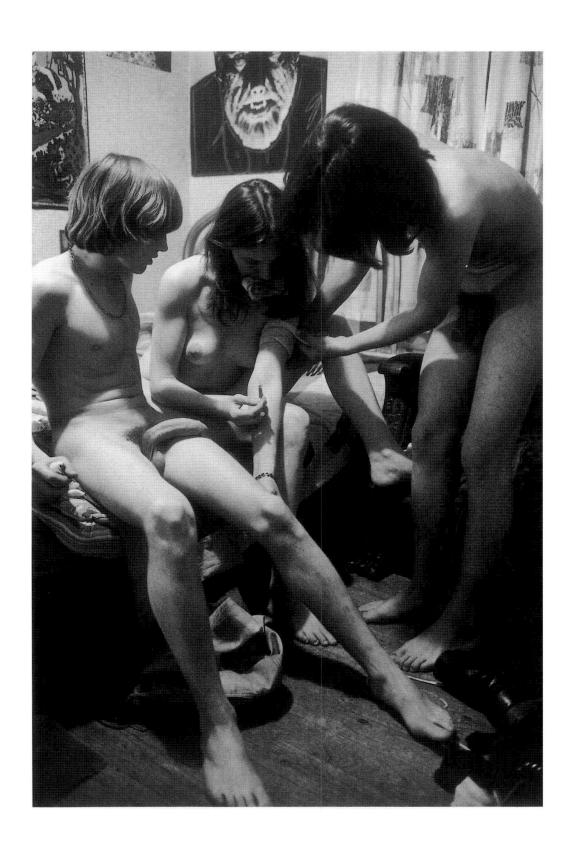

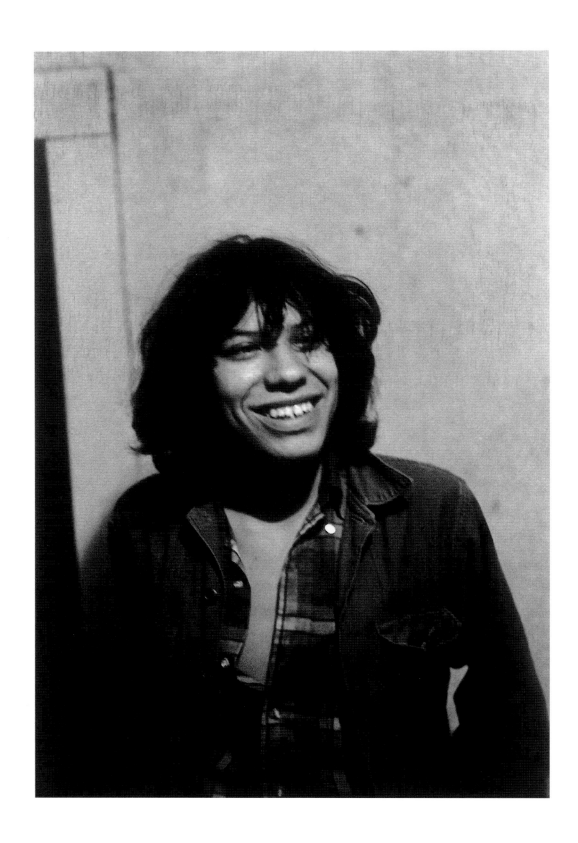

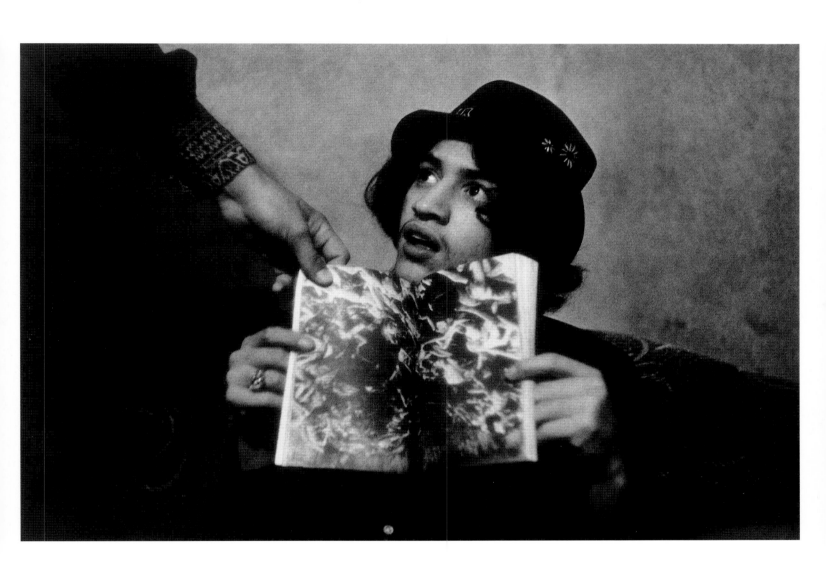

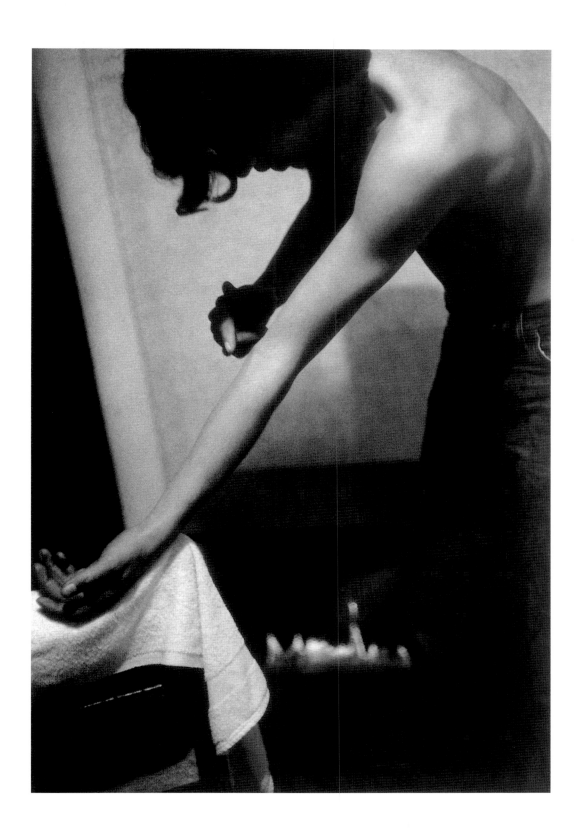